songs of youth

a collection of poetry

by Téa Nicolae.

table of contents

foreword

teenage angst

    i. of wildness

    ii. of jumbled warmth

    iii. of the world

    iv. of shame

my loss is my root

    of grief

at last, light

    of joy

foreword

The one consistency in my life, from childhood to the teenage years of angst and to the blooms of young adulthood, has been writing. I wrote to make sense of the world around me and of myself, I wrote to express myself, I wrote to connect to the world and to myself.

This is a collection of poetry written between the ages of sixteen and twenty. Brian Molko of Placebo, who was the soundtrack to my teenage years and the one who hypnotised me with rawness and alluring born-to-die sadness, once said that, when you are a teenager, you react to the world that surrounds you with great emotionality and intensity, with full heart. He mused that growing older is a process of finding semblances of sanity. This collection aims to illustrate exactly that; it is not written by an adult looking back with maturity, nor tenderness to their early years, but by the teenager who is in the midst of experiencing the turbulent highs and lows of being thrown into life.

This collection of poetry was a creative project I compiled as an undergraduate student of Creative Writing at

Lancaster University. It includes unpublished work, as well as work that has already been published. It is structured in three sections: 'teenage angst', 'my loss is my root' and 'at last, light', which chronicle the journey to adulthood through churn, grief, and joy.

You may notice that the poetry is written in lowercase. More than an aesthetic choice, lowercase marks the teenage search for identity and reflects how disconnected teenagers feel to themselves. As a teenager myself, I found it difficult to capitalise 'I'-s, as it seemed as if I was proclaiming who I was before I knew. This collection explores the beginning of the search for the 'I'.

Enjoy.

teenage angst

i. of wildness

ii. of jumbled warmth

iii. of the world

iv. of shame

i. of wildness

i untangle my youth

i untangle my youth
in wild cities that make me squirm
thirstily clinging
to fruit flavoured wine
and burning my tongue
with round-shaped pills

i feel the party to my core
i dance violently
contorting my limbs
to trivial dance anthems
i throw myself
against my friends' bodies
hungry for emptied affection

when i shut my eyes
i float

as the bass the drums the music

flow through my veins

and strengthen my bones

at closing time

we leave the dance floor

holding hands

whispering untold truths

with damp cheeks

i tremble in my oversized coat

but i relish the warmth

in our laced fingers

5:11 in the morning

we dance on the westminster bridge

spiralling in sequins

i stretch my arms and roll my head

and the stars are closer

i twirl and i wish

i could cradle them in my hand

the ferris wheel glows
and my friends sparkle
and i want to glue their faces
to my mind

my best friend turns to me
sweaty
with a glimmer in his eyes
and chewing on a cigarette
'i wish my mother
could be this happy'
he says with adoration
and
i cry.

(*published in tastzine, 2019).

i wrap my sadness in sequins

i wrap my sadness in sequins.

i pour my sadness in fake eyelashes,

in glitter nails,

in green hair dye,

and i take my sadness out for a dance.

flash lights,

spilled drinks,

heels that crush your toes.

i lock hands with my sadness

and sway on sticky dance floors.

my sadness holds up her pocket mirror

in grimy club bathrooms

and she puts on three layers of red lipstick

while i rub off mine.

i ask my sadness to pull up my torn zipper

while, pupils enlarged,

i hum stevie nicks adoringly.

i throw a clumsy arm over my sadness

and guide her to another club.

i grind on empty party anthems

and, when boys try to kiss me,

i brush them off

because i'm loyal to my sadness.

at the end of the night

i stuff my face with my sadness

and we hail a cab in silence.

home,

my sadness whispers gutted love declarations to me

and tucks me in my bed gently.

(*a lengthened version of this poem was published in cake magazine, 2019).

my youth spills

on dance floors

pitch-black clubs,

dazed fridays.

my youth pumps

through my veins.

high heels,

shiny fake ids.

my youth grounds me.

sticky dance floors,

my youth bursts inside of me

it glides through me

wildly

as my heart throbs

beneath my skin

matching the music's beat

i please my youth

bending my body obediently

with the deafening bass

midnight

the synth dismantles my mind

and my limbs

are not mine anymore

they follow the sound

there is no past

or future

only my body

spinning madly

only the music

twisting in my ears

only my youth

spilling on dance floors

from the crashed bottles of wine

at my feet

(*published in kamena magazine,

2022).

space monkey

*urban dictionary: space monkey is a game usually played by teens, where a person either chokes themselves or has someone else do it to them until they almost pass out. it can cause brain damage to the lack of oxygen to the brain.

every time i feel ugly,

i pull my hair out of my roots and play space monkey with the boy that lives two streets down from me.

we meet in his room at 11pm,

usually on tuesdays.

we order taco bell

and choke each other

with greasy fingers.

i find solace in his grasp.

the harsher he gets,

the more beautiful i am.

necks clenched, we stare in silence,

and i remember the nights i spent on bathroom floors

drunk, wondering what broke me.

i'd tell my boy

about my bathroom nights,

but we never speak.

we just clutch our throats

and collapse into each other,

cat scars on our arms

lapsing back into old habits.

we spend four nights a month and forty-eight a year

gazing at our draining cheeks

and drowning into each other.

i know each one of his pimples,

his chapped puckered lips,

his clumsily shaved sideburns

and the straight slope of his nose,

while he knows the mole in my left eyebrow,

and sees the cracks in my oil-based foundation.

when his fingers close around my neck,

he understands me,

just like children understand the world with their hands.

when we fall into each other,

breathless,

with fragments of dream buzzes burning our heads,

the lack of oxygen strips our minds bare,

and i am beautiful again.

(*published in flash journal, 2018).

gasping for air in my bell jar,

i long for closure
and i crave familiarity,
melded thoughts and warm hands.

i am desperate to connect.
i want to feel someone's soul
glued to mine.

i dream of intimacy,
but i'm clumsy:
when people embrace me too tightly,
i hiss like a cornered snake.

i'm wary of being alone, but
i drift away during conversations,
i ignore messages,
i break friendships,

i feign smiles.

i find refuge

in my bell jar.

every night

i close the jar's lid with shaky hands,

hug my knees

and blow air on the glass.

(*published in scan journal, 2020).

ii. of jumbled warmth

you said you loved me accusatorily

with a glimmer in your eyes.

your hands entwined with mine
like ivy,
swiftly travelled to my shoulders
and strangled my neck
with care.

your tender messages were
sweet like thyme
and your love
smothered me.

i was ashamed
that i could not mirror your affection,
but God knows i tried.

on our last night together

you listened to music

while i cried on the floor.

as you slept,

i curled to the edge of your bed.

lips pressed to my knees,

i saw through my attachment to you,

and left wordlessly.

i know i did you wrong, too,

i'm sorry.

but love does not cage.

you only wrote

about sex and death

and i wrote about birth and pain.

in our days of yore,

you took me to graveyards,

took photos of my bare back

while we listened to velvet underground.

when i was told you broke off your engagement,

i thought about

calling you

and found comfort in the fantasy

of holding each other at dawn,

forgetting where one ends

and where the other begins.

that night,

i ruined my mascara at my kitchen table,

remembering your voice,

reading me a poem about the death of your mother,

remembering your eyes,

gazing softly as i crumbled.

yet you only wrote about sex and death,

and i wrote about birth and pain.

it would never work,

i told myself,

and cried in a hotel room in lisboa

face down on a duvet that smelled like the sea.

love in the age of social media

i think i wish i knew
what you've been reading,
what bands you're into
and what dreams you're weaving. (?)

it's been one year and a half
since you've unfollowed me on instagram
and i've deleted you on facebook.
i miss you. (?)

i wonder if you wish you knew
that i'm writing again
that i dyed my hair
that i wear black lipstick and gold hoops.

i haven't unblocked you out of prideful frailty

but i've conscientiously kept up the virtual appearances

one is lured to, follow parting.

i made up with the right friends,

posted pretty selfies,

changed my make-up just rightly.

i smiled widely in pictures

and avoided sharing sad poetry.

but you don't know.

you don't know that

i was torn the other day

that i changed therapists

that i'm playing keyboards in a rock band

yesterday,

my friend sent me a screenshot

of your new profile picture.

you looked good.

healthy and polished,

probably my opposite these days.

and you don't know

that i sway to heartbreak pop at midnight

that i lost my mother's ring

that on one cold night in london i sat
beneath the twinkling lights and i thought

i knew who i was

i think i miss you,

but i've almost forgotten you.

i haven't read your carefully written captions

and i haven't seen your moles in over a year.

erasing each other from our social media

was a cleansing process.

i can't even remember why we drifted apart.

i'm just pissed that you haven't seen me blossoming,

because you unfollowed me on instagram.

and you won't ever know

that i quit drinking coffee

that i learnt to swim

that i threw myself in the sea, wearing the dress you liked,

and the dress stuck to my thighs

and for once

i ceased to feel unwanted

like your casual distance used to make me feel.

when i met you

i

was

quiet

because

i

was

writing

a poem

to

you

inside

my

head.

(*published in scan journal, 2020).

throes

you

spilled ice cream on my sundress

and swayed me to rock ballads

i

reminded you of spring

and faded in the summer breeze

we

had a common affinity

for boys with smudged eyes dressed in pretty skirts

singing scratchy songs about loves lost to heroin

you

were my stained musician

i

was your absentminded poetess

we

were seeking to destroy ourselves

for throes of applause and tastes of success

you

did.

i

was one step before the chasm

when stratospheric glooms parted.

i

suddenly knew

that my quill did not have to be my ruin.

i

suddenly saw

that i could create beauty.

my hands are still warm

from when you held them between yours.
i was cold,
and ached to be
smart and pretty.

i wondered
if you could see right through me,
and veiled my cheeks in my hair

i see right through me.

kiss me

i'm peaking

you murmur

lips pressed

against

my

forehead

i look up

to you

your eyeballs

are shaking

your hair

is

damp

and

you look

so

beautiful

i feel

my eyes

rolling to

the back

of

my head

as i crash

my mouth

to yours

my hands

fall

on your

chest

and

i feel

your warmth

slip

through

my skin

wrapping

my heart

your hands

rest on

my waist

your beard

scratches

my ear

and i feel

tangled

with you

my mouth

is

dry

and

the

music

is

tearing

my

chest

open

i

feel

dizzy

i bring

your

hands

to

my

heart

do

you

feel this

your voice

is hoarse

you

are

holding

my

youth

between

your

fingertips

i nod

is it

love

i

don't

know

but

i

feel

so

close

to you

right

now

(*published in

the writing disorder, 2020).

mi amor no tiene esperanza

cold cups of coffee
on my nightstand
you lick my neck
dawn unfolds softly

my lips trace your forearm
you nudge my cheek, our
eyes lock. your bright teeth
dazzle, morning's charm

i bury my head in your chest
you hum a silky tune as your
fingers run through my hair,
hand clasped on my breast

i could get used to tasting
the coffee in your mouth

i think; the sun is pouring
down, our legs are lacing

i want to ask you to stay,
but i can't. our love, soft
in daylight, would slowly
crumble in layers of grey

if you do. it'd bear its teeth,
slicing our folded skin
into bite-sized pieces,
stripping tenderness of shield

we melt differently,
i decide, as your phone
sings a love-sick spanish
melody from your spotify

you wear leather shoes,

i dance bare foot. you're
chasing paper, i'm humbly
writing about my blues

querido, you must go
and i'll remember
our warm hands. caramel
coffee, sweet summer flow

your eyes are calm
my heart flourishes
and i press my cheek
against your palm

so long,
mi amor

[untitled]

(it is spring), i miss

your damp forehead

between my shoulder blades

(i can't bear to look at the moon again); i miss

how you used to bite my earlobe

whenever i drifted away

[or whenever i picked up

books like

the hundred thousand songs of milarepa

because

poetry more beautiful than ours

gave you a headache]

(my darling), i miss

your firm grasp

on my hips

(i've been sleeping on your side); i miss

how your eyes

used to   soften

when i sang

ballads to the   cosmos,

wearing your duvet as the high priestesses of athena

would have worn their robes

[and when you looked at me with adoration i felt like an enchantress ,,,,, dazzling, alive, fire in my belly, a daughter of the seas ,,,,,, and i conjured all the elements in the texture of our lips]

(i'm sorry i promised to visit but i didn't) i miss

curling up to you

sweaty hearts pressed together,

your fingertips drawing

stars and suns on my back;;;

the night i left you

i laid awake

locking eyes with the night sky

through your half-opened window,

i was cold and

i wiped my tears on your pillow case.

at one-point i could have sworn

the sky slipped into your chamber

and laid in bed with us

and i thought

etcetera.

(*published in
the writing disorder, 2020).

iii. of the world

when the last tree burns

and the last drop of water falls

when the soil dries and crumbles

and the Earth's womb shrivels

when loss swells in the air

and death curls in the dust

there will be no one left to murmur

forgive us, Mother,

for defiling you.

(*published in balkan beats, 2020).

layla curled her hair when she was sad

layla curled her hair when she was sad

and picked at her food with clumsy fingers

'one more bite',

i used to urge,

and she would shake her head with a smile.

layla counted the calories in her food when she was sad.

'i think i've lost weight again', she would say,

looking at her feet.

i counted how many crisps she'd had in my head

as she pushed her food with her fork.

layla wrote poems when was sad.

when she read me a poem she wrote about food,

i wished she craved to fill herself

with the gentleness she carried for others.

layla cried when she was sad

and i held her tightly.

'why do i treat myself so horribly'

she once whispered in my hair.

when layla was told that she would end up in hospital

if she lost more weight

she vowed to be as kind to herself

as she was to others.

she struggled for four months

to fight her mind and her belly

and she cried and hurt

as i stared helplessly.

but when she picked herself up

she held her head high,

like a warrior.

today layla curls her hair when she feels grateful

and sends me photos of clean plates.

she tells me she feels hunger

with bright eyes

'i've never felt hungry before.

now i crave hot-boiled potatoes.'

'i felt full

because i fed my brain the wrong things.'

she tells me softly

as pride floods my heart.

afterschool

11:29, local coffeeshop.

spoonful of fruitcake,

david bowie is dead.

phone buzz,

there's a lump in my throat.

when will you be home?

if the greats ash to dust like funk to funky,

to which blackstar do the rest us go?

i hold my breath my cappuccino went cold.

iv. of shame

a million stories

chastised: rotten, fallen.

sinful, impure.

blackened eyes, bleeding thighs, chipped teeth,

my country holds a million stories

of a woman's tears.

i used to think i came from a country

where women were expected to stay silent,

yet i came to see that a country is a country is a country

until its women stand.

shame

is learned.

the thirty-ninth time

i felt ashamed

to be female was

when you strangled my shoulders

with your right arm

in the back of a dimly-lit pub,

where i was sipping my white russian

quietly.

you stared at my chest

with a foul grin

and i fidgeted,

wishing i didn't have breasts.

i swatted your hand away softly

and moved closer to my friend,

who was lying on her side,

smoking shisha.

you followed me

when i stepped outside for fresh air.

my heels weighed me down

and you put your hand

on my back and said

'i've got you'.

'i've got myself',

i cut you off

and reached for my friend.

on the dance floor, i swayed

while you leered at me.

when you put your hands

on my waist

i pushed you off

and you grabbed my arm harshly,

digging your curly fingers

into my skin.

i twitched.

'let go.'

i hissed.

you did.

the next day

you called me a whore,

while your friends snickered.

there were violet traces on my arm.

my loss is my root
of grief

loss slithered inside me

like a snake,
slicing my bones
and scratching my veins
with its scales.

my loss
burnt my fingertips
and dug a hole
in the centre of my chest.

i tried to feed the hole
kindness, drugs, and love
but my loss swallowed it all
and hungrily pushed against my ribs.

when i'm quiet
i can hear the hole

swelling under my heart,

greedily.

(*featured in wretched city,

2021).

my hips are bruised
in my dreams

my hips are bruised in my dreams
and i wake up itching,
pressing my fingers onto my thighs,
covering my purple skin.

my hips swell in my dreams
and tentacles circle my feet,
wrapping around my toes when i walk
and i stumble and fall on my face.
when i wake up,
my cheeks ache.

my wrists are blistered in my dreams
and there is ash under my fingernails.
when i wake up,
my hands are swollen.

on cold nights

when i'm afraid to go to sleep

i light three candles

and hug my knees.

i promise myself

that one day

i won't dream of bruises

one day

my dreams will be amber

and i'll wake up with warmth

in my stomach.

(*a version of this poem was published in eunoia review, 2019).

of when my brain

curled into itself

and everything was numb

and nothing hurt

0.25mg

doses: three

day: one

swallow first dose

conscientiously

at 8:54

in the morning

side effects:

forgetfulness

roll in sheets, pat the mattress, search for phone

trembling

double-press snooze

changes in patterns

fall on back in bed, bring knees to chest

clumsiness and unsteadiness

doze off

drowsiness

jerk as the alarm goes off

feeling sad and empty

snooze snooze snooze

shakiness, an unsteady walk

rub eyes. small ache in the back of head. feels like it's melting thoughts apart.

slurred speech

jump as the alarm rings for the third time.

(less common side effects:)

loss of self-control

search for a pair of panties to match mood. grey

loss of coordination

pull shirt over head

loss of memory

flatten the wrinkles with hands

loss of voice

apply foundation unevenly

muscle stiffness

press nose to mirror. stare at glazed eyes. swallow.

it is indeed true

that my brain curled into itself

and everything was numb and nothing hurt.

yet while my insides didn't clench anymore

my eyes could still see

the hurt.

(*a version of this poem was published in L.C., 2018).

my loss is my root

my loss is my root

when my legs are wobbly.

it keeps me level-headed, grounded,

with my feet turned inward.

my loss is motherly. it keeps me nurtured, well fed, full.

my loss is nourishing, it wets my lips when my mouth is dry.

on good days,

i like to think that

my loss blossoms in my core

and drops through my feet to the moist soil

it falls to the centre of the earth,

through tangled grass

and layers of rock

it feeds on flower stems, leaves, seeds,

and absorbs the warmth of mother earth.

when it skyrockets back to me,

it throbs with energy

it heals my body and patches the open wounds in my brain.

on good days,

i imagine my loss sprinkling the ground like rain.

it wets my fingers, and when i cry,

the soil thrives.

(*published in litehouse, 2020).

i dream

that my teeth fall out at night

i dream

that my teeth fall out at night

and i swallow them,

one by one.

my teeth scratch the insides

of my throat

and i choke on them.

i wake up crying,

cover my mouth and scream into my fingers,

pushing my hands into my forehead,

as if i'm trying to pull my mind

out of my head.

i am crying all the time now.

i cry in the shower

i cry in front of my untouched breakfast

i cry in toilets in metro stations

i cry gracelessly doing my make-up

i cry when i wash my hair with blueberry shampoos

i cry when i read your messages,

the 67th time.

i cry and i long for you,

i cry and i long for you.

some days

i cry less and i eat apples

some days

i wear red and buy you flowers.

some days

my mind blocks my pain

and i am better.

some days

my friends make me laugh

and i find comfort in being alive.

i dread those days.

those days my head swims in guilt

and my shame thumps in my ears.

those days i feel myself forgetting you

and i wish i could glue your eyes to my mind.

when those days end,

i break my mind with photos of you

and i dream of melting.

dearest,

i'm soaking in loss

and i'm chanting buddhist mantras

they say that i should surrender my grief

they say that we are bound together,

even if i heal

but how can it be

when you only exist through my pain

dearest,

i am willing to suffer each day for you

so you do not to die again.

(*a version of this poem was published in the Lancashire Literary Award anthology and was subsequently shortlisted for the LLA prize in 2019).

letters, cuts

01. 01. 2016.

dearest,

it's been one month.

i miss you.

01. 11. 2016.

darling,

when i couldn't sleep at night,

i used to write letters to allen ginsberg in my head.

now i only write letters to you.

i write soft letters on mondays,

pained letters on tuesdays

and longing letters on saturdays.

my writing is cursive, inclined to the right

and my s's are round and deep.

you never respond,

not even in my mind.

15. 12. 2016.

beloved,

i think i'm better,

my mind is gentler.

it terrifies me,

so, on good days,

i dig my nails into my palm

and tear at my arms until my shirt is moist.

on bad days,

loss chews on the layers of my skin

and i want to peel them off

before it eats through me.

10. 01. 2017.

dearest,

i cried for one week when david bowie died.

i wish i could have held your hand

when i read the news.

i wish we could have ran barefoot

on your favourite streets at midnight

laughing with fresh teeth.

i wish you could have screamed in my left
ear: *'gee, my life's a funny thing, am i still
too young?'*

16. 08. 2017.

dear,

i'm unsure where loss ends

and i begin.

26. 09. 2017.

my one,

i am better.

i keep my nails trimmed

and clutch my loss to my chest,

motherly.

28. 09. 2017.

ever dearest,

i've been reading about the cycle of rebirth

i wish to believe in it,

but scepticism clouds my heart.

i'm not pure enough for transcendence

so if i am reborn

i wish i could be as small

as a sparrow.

11. 01. 2018.

dear one,

i wear my loss

like i wear my rings.

30. 10. 2018.

i wish there were folders of you in my brain.

i wish i could revisit all my memories with you,

choose and freeze shots of you.

19. 02. 2019.

my one,

i hope you are well,

i hope you are nestled warmly.

i miss you.

> *(*fragments of this sequence of poems were published in scan journal, 2020).*

it's been three years

and i swear i am trying.

i bought a shiny yoga mat

and i do yin yoga for grief release.

i ground my feet,

do warrior poses

and chant.

i try,

but no matter

how much i contort my body at dawn

sorrow rips through my brain

and sticks to my eyelids.

i swear i'm trying.

i've stopped reading sylvia plath

and i bookmark poems

that say there's a universe inside me.

i read self-help articles

about how everything happens for a reason,

grinding my teeth.

i write inspirational quotes

on purple notebooks

and make bullet-points about buddhism

with pink pens.

i press the tips onto the paper

hard

as if to push what i write through me.

i beg my mind to meditate

i put on compilations of meditation music

instant relief from anxiety & stress.

deep relaxing & healing music

and i force myself to still.

i download apps that ease anxiety

and i go to meditation groups

on wednesdays.

but no matter how long i stay

cross-legged on the floor,

straightening my back

and linking my thumbs,

it hurts.

dearest,

i quit drinking

and i made new friends.

friends that drink hot chocolate,

watch soft films

friends that pray in the evenings

friends that don't drown in techno music

friends that don't sprawl

themselves on dance floors

or swallow pills

friends that meet for coffee and talk about how simple life is

and i nod when my heart clenches.

i tried to spill out my loss

i. on the 15th of september

grief wrote me a song

and

i can't remember the first chords.

ii. my brain

is softly melting to the floor

iii. i write about the face of grief

so i don't forget

the curve of grief's neck

her sharp teeth

your unevenly cut hair

and his faint eyeliner.

iv. i dream of unzipping my veins

and of plunging into nothingness,

but fear holds me by my hair,

up in the air,

neck bent.

v. when i was fourteen

i dreamt of being famous

of having my face plastered on shiny books.

now i just want it to stop hurting

i would give it all,

if it stopped hurting.

all my phony achievements,

all my lousy dreams.

vi. i search for

kind songs for lonely people

on youtube

to fall asleep.

vii. i am

a caricature of an empty person

that tries to be good.

i am terrified of being found out.

i cry in taxis,

i break in front of mirrors.

i am unkind

and i hide it well.

i try

i

try.

i carry oversized gift bags

on the bus

and hang torn earphones

from my neck.

chin stuck to ice smudged windows,

i hum of make-believe merriment

and rip price tags smoothly.

i

try.

i fold myself in silk ribbons

and curl my yore

in matching jumpers

i paint my face in red and green

and break two fingers

flattening pink wish cards.

i crunch on gingerbread

and choke on warmth at noon.

i

try.

i eat cold pizza

and squint at christmas rom-coms

in the mornings

i munch on burnt popcorn

and adorn plastic trees at midnights,

gracelessly.

i watch friends unwrap my presents

and rest my forehead

on their shoulders

how did you know?

they kiss my hair

this is the best gift i've ever got

i

try.

i fly home

i cry on the plane

i smile at my mother

i crumble in my room

i try.

i am insomniac and slippery

but i try.

(*published in L.C., 2017).

my loss

used to burn

the roof

of my mouth.

i breathed it every morning,

and when i pushed it

with my tongue,

it glued to my teeth.

i tried to swallow my loss,

but it got stuck

in my throat

and stifled my voice.

so.

i had to thrust

my arm down my neck.

i dreamed of grief

every night

but i had to. (forgive me)

i had to

plunge

my nails

into my loss.

i wrote letters

to grief's phantom

every day,

but i had to

rip it out,

i had to

rip it out.

stretching

my arm,

i did not dare

to look,

but i felt

my loss pulsing

in my hands,

meaty, bloody, engorging,

and i lifted it up

to the heavens.

i sang my loss

and i howled my love

to the skies

and

i

surrendered.

i had to.

i loved you

dearly,

my darling grief,

but i had to.

i had to

i had to

i had to

i had to

i had to

i had to

i had to

　　　　　　sonnet　sorrow
　　　　　　　brief　　　to

　　　　　　　　　I
　　　　　　　　　　　am
　　　　　　　digesting
　　　　　　　　　　my
　　　　　　　　　　　　loss
　　　　　　　　　　　as
　　　　　　　　　　　　　life
　　　　　　　　　dances
　　　　　　　　　　　　on
　　　　　　　　　　　　　　the
　　　　　　　　　　　　　tip
　　　　　　　　　　　　　　　of
　　　　　　　　　　　　　my
　　　　　　　　tongue

(published in the writing disorder, 2020).

when   loss burns   sharply
        my   too
i curve   fingers   my chest
       my   into
and i rip it
       out.
i fold my   in   napkins,
      loss   lilac
i   it in my pocket
  stuff
and i run,
bare foot.

i run
until   nails
   my   crack,
and   toes
   my   bleed.

and
    i
      stand.
i wipe   with the back
    my tears   of my hand
and
    i
      stretch
myself   the
      to   sky,
spine   twisting,
bones   ticking   out
of   my   skin,
and   blow   the
    i   out   sky.

when   open   mouth
    i   my

    the   and   moon
       stars   the
sizzle   in   my   teeth

  grinning
i   take   my   loss
out   of   my pocket

and   knit   in   sky
   i   it   the
and   loss   brighter   the
   my   shines   than
                      moon

at last, light

of joy

Ānanda

i allow myself
    to feel joy,
  peeling carrots
with my grandmother,
  stroking my nose
    against my doe rabbit's

i allow myself
    to feel beauty,
  adorning my neck
with rose quartz necklaces,
  gazing at the night sky
    sliding itself into dawn

i allow myself
    to feel stillness,
laying my naked skin
  in fresh lavender sheets,
    placing hands on my belly,
      counting eleven deep breaths

i allow myself
    to feel grief,
embellishing my knees
  with tears, planting kisses
    on the blisters
      that bejewel my skin

   i allow myself
      to twinkle alive,
  tulle pressed
    to my damp thighs,
      dancing with my
         hands above my head

i
  allow
life
  to flow
    through
      me

(*published in 'get well soon' zine, 2020).

i breathe,

i accept my grief

i wake up at dawn

and i find happiness

in slicing an apple

and munching on it

breathe

i accept my grief

i find beauty

in standing barefoot

in the middle of the kitchen,

feeling breadcrumbs stick

to my pinky toe

i breathe

i accept my grief

i learn there is joy in cutting tomatoes,

in making a bowl of soup,

in having my stomach full

breathe

i accept my grief

i uncover the childish glee of

having the tip of my tongue burnt

and gratitude runs between my fingers

like water

being alive is warm

there is kindness

in tuning in

and

i breathe

i accept

my

grief. ☼

(*published in scan journal, 2020).

times i felt fleeting traces of joy

When:

1. my friend put her head in my lap

    underneath a colossal tree. it was

    pouring hard

    and our minds were melting ((infused with divine moments of truth))

    pupils dilated, she said: 'i never imagined i would be so connected to anyone

    as i am to you'

    i stroked her hair

    tears fell down my neck

2. my rabbit nudged my cheeks with her wet nose

    as i cried and prayed to the Divine Mother

    and i curled my fingers in her soft fur

    and she purred.

3. caught the 5 a.m. train with my friends
   running on the slippery platform,
   bare foot. dirt sticking to my toes
   tripping in my long dress,
   beaming

4. (i was) awkwardly kissed in the middle of
   the sidewalk, hand cradling my neck
   we parted,,, laughed til our bellies hurt
   his cheeks flushed
   i held his hand between mine
   (and we walked in silence)

5. drops of rain hit my face in berlin
   as i danced frantically, high;;
   my mouth was smiling
   my insides were smiling

5. i felt deliciously beautiful

twirling in my rainbow tutu crocheted by my sister for the parade

sparkly stars on my eyelids on the top of my lips

love bubbling in my chest

7. i slipped out of your bed,

    tip-toeing to the door but you grabbed my waist,

    pleaded (i) stay(ed)

    and i did.

    your kisses were tender, your feet were cold, you drooled in your sleep

    and i was too jolly to close my eyelids

    so i drew constellations on your sheets with my fingernails

8. i burnt my tongue

    taking a big bite

    of the first dish i ever cooked

    i called my grandma with my mouth full

and she giggled

9. fingers touching the cold shiny surface of my mirror,

    i placed a kiss on my lips as if to say

    'I love you. I'm sorry I've been mistreating you.'

10. my grandma caressed my hair

    as the sun beat down on our backs

    in relentless waves

    her knees smelled like my childhood

11. i held hands with my sisters in the temple

    seated in a circle with flowers in our hair,
    eyes closed, softly chanting to the Goddess

    and for the first time in my life, i felt [deeply,

    thoroughly]

    LOVED. [* AND not for the idea of me, but for who I truly AM.]

you can taste the world

forty-five minutes

for the first time in your life

you can taste the world

you can taste

the sunlight creeping through your window

and the wind blowing through you

you can taste the pulse of the universe

it tastes like cut-up paper

with a hint of bitter ink

one hour and a half

your cheeks flush

your mind spins

as reality wavers

deep breaths

your eyes marvel

as if you've never seen before

you run your hands through your hair

it feels like sand

and

it crumbles under your touch

two hours and a half, peak

you are sweating

you press your fingers onto your forehead

it seems elastic

and you wonder if

your fingers could

enter your skull

you imagine

holding your mind in your hands

and reading it like a book

you tremble at the thought

and clutch your hands together

to stop them from wandering

seven hours

gratitude washes over you

you are thankful for your knees

for your fingernails

for your chest

for your mother

who carried you in her womb

with care

you are grateful for love

and for the bliss that swirls on your tongue

you are thankful for the life

that blossoms in your core

eight hours

you place your hand on your heart

its pounding quietens your mind

and you feel your body throbbing

in waves of life

this is the sound of existence

you think

a beating, meaty heart

meditation attempt

i imagine a round ball of warmth and light
that fills my brain
my belly
my legs
and my fingernails
with softness

it warms the bottom of my feet
travels to my ankles tenderly
and softens the muscles in my thighs
it spirals around my stomach
and rests on my shoulders

as the golden ball
is about to engulf my insides
every time
like clockwork

my brain fidgets

and longs for the wonder

of the outside world

pierced with restlessness

the ball of warmth and light

crumbles

i try to lure it back into my mind

desperately

i keep my eyes shut

but my fingers wander on their own

lunging and grabbing

for what they can reach

and i am but a child again

trying to understand the world

with my hands.

ode to poems lost

[on the cutting board]

to my poems of diffidence

to my poems of cruelty

to my poems of hurt

to my poems of shame

to my poems of anger

to my poems of frailty

i welcome you

i cradle you

yet i've been holding onto you

for far too long.

too much of me fell in shame

of my womb and breasts

too much of me fell

in the knife-burn of anger

too much of me fell

in spelling cruelties with my tongue

too much of me fell

in holding onto bruised tears

enough.

at last, light.

i sip hastily.

stanzas on pulsation

where does   sadness   come from

i wonder, tracing my fingertips over my body

here?

i tap my forehead

here?

i run my hands through my hair

here?

i elongate my cheeks

      here?

i strangle my neck

        here?

i fold my arms together

here?

i lay my palms flat on my heart space

here?

i extend my legs

here?

i stretch my toes

here?

i press my fingers against my ankles

what about   here?

i place my hands on my womb

FIRE

i scream

    FIRE as SADNESS
sprawls from my cervix

FIRE as SADNESS
shoots up my body

    FIRE as white flames
burn my central channel

FIRE as SADNESS skyrockets to my
    crown and falls back to my cervix

fire as my womb
    confides in me

    fire as she enumerates
the afternoons

   i starved her

the wounds dug
  into her thighs

the tears of exhaustion
shed when she needed

rest

fire as she recalls the fingers
      that stifled her voice

  the lovers that
choked her mind

  the curled fists
dug into her ligaments

the spite i have been feeding her

i

    i   i

    i   i   i

cry   apologize   beg

    am   cry
    accept

        terrified

my

.

                penance

.

.

.

.

.

LIGHT i scream as rays of
sunlight gush from my cervix

LIGHT pulsing through, mending
the body as it soars to my crown

LIGHT cascading down, back
to my cervix encompassing my

being in loving awareness
as my womb forgives me

and i melt
my face

my arms
my nails

strands of my hair

moles on my chest

melt in the
pools of my

womb which is
ignited with

the flow
of pure

LO
VE

warmth drips from my
eye to my root and

there's

only

LIGHT

        LIGHT

LIGHT

            LIGHT

        LIGHT

i teach myself to love

on early sunday mornings,
when the sun is gentle
and my feet are cold.

i dip my fingertips in morning dew
and count
the things i hate about myself
in a loving manner.
my nose, my chin, my loss,
my nose, my chin, my loss,
my nose, my chin, my loss

.

.

.

i murmur,
endlessly,
until the words

are as smooth as velvet in my mouth

and my hatred makes me giggle.

my nose, my chin, my loss

i gaze at myself

through my cracked phone screen

and i cradle my face

as gently as my mother would.

my nose, my chin, my loss

i touch my nose

and my chin,

feeling my skin soften

beneath my fingers.

i ache

pressing my fingers on my ribcage,

i touch my loss.

it's moist like the grass

that curls around my toes,

it's fleshy,

like a round plume.

i love

sunrise in my hair,

i stir beneath the crisp morning light

and find

there is delicacy

in my most loathed parts.

i ache

love exists.

i feel it,

pouring through my veins,
rich and heavy.

for a fraction of a second,
i climb so close to myself
and i love
gently,
dearly,
completely.

it's an early sunday morning
and i *love*.

spring song

holding my sisters' hands

between mine

i sing to the little girl

who stumbled her way to the woman i am.

i sing to the glee

i felt on my first bleed, carefully arranging my pad on my panties,

wondering 'am i a woman now?' with a puffed chest

and i sing to the shame

my mother taught me,

i sing to my blood becoming an untold secret shackled between my legs.

i sing to the sweet joy

that came with buying my first pink bra,

a fusion of tiny bows and flower petals

and i sing to hearing a woman
declare on television
that breasts that looked like mine were
'just wrong'.

i sing to the desire for acceptance
that throbbed inside of me
when i heard the girls in my class tease those whose hair adorned their legs

and i sing to the blood
that stained my stockings
when i clumsily shaved my legs
with my father's razor. i cut my skin,
and the sting lasted for days.

i sing to my first lover,

to the ache between my legs

and to the blood on his right thigh,

to his sweet smile and to our entangled hands

and i sing to the taint

that spoiled the memory,

being called a whore by a friend of a friend
of a friend.

i sing to my small voice that whispered

me too

and i sing to my christening on the internet.

when the gentle arms of my sisters lock
around me, our tears merge together, and our
stories intertwine in one.

my stifled voice rushes forward, my shame
trickles into sweetness

and i sing to shying away from women,

to being afraid to open my heart

and i sing to disrobing the shyness,
to stepping into the circle of women
and to drinking
the grace that ripples through.
i sing to being nourished by the success,
grace and power of the women in my life
i sing to being held, loved, and seen

and i caress the shame the little girl felt
letting it blossom in the palms of my hands,
pouring loving awareness
into the wounds stored within my body
until my heart releases and pulses
with pride
in the light of sovereignty

and

my little girl is lovingly held

by my woman.

acknowledgements

My deepest gratitude to my family, friends, and teachers, who continuously shower me with immeasurable support, care, and guidance. Hearty thanks are due to my parents, who unshakingly and lovingly support me on my path both as a writer and as a seeker, even when my journey appears strange or foreign to them. A special thank you to Holly Robinson, who did me the great honour of gracing me with her talent by creating the incredibly beautiful cover art of my collection. Profound thanks to my professors, tutors, and Creative Writing colleagues, who diligently help me in honing my writing skills and in expanding my understanding of literature, as well as my vision of myself as a writer. Each of you have supported me in stepping into the woman that I am today. Words fail short.

Finally, a deep thank you to the readers of this collection. I am incredibly honoured that you chose to spend your time reading my words.

All my love.

about the author

Téa Nicolae is a Romanian poetess and scholar-practitioner living in the United Kingdom. She holds a B.A. in Film and Creative Writing and an M.A. in Religious Studies from Lancaster University. She is currently completing her second M.A. in the Writing of Poetry and Literary Translation at Warwick University and will soon commence a Ph.D. at Edinburgh University with a thesis centred on the Indian epic poem the *Mahābhārata*. Téa writes devotional (*bhakti*) poetry as well as confessional poetry, and her main research interests are the *Mahābhārata*, Śāktism, and non-dual philosophy.

Cover art by Holly Robinson.